VE MAR 2015
SU Oct 17

Editing:
it's Time for Correckshuns!

written by Terri Kelley
illustrated by Milena Radeva

Copyright © 2013, Terri Kelley
All rights reserved. No copies may be made of this book without
the written permission from the author.
ISBN-13:978-1482549423
ISBN-10:1482549425

Sunshine Press
www.sunshinepress.net

*Be sure to check for discounted packages when ordering all of the
Writing is a Process books (a series of eight books in all).
School personnel and other educational organizations should contact Terri Kelley
at her website*
www.terriLkelley.com
*to inquire about bulk discounts available
when purchases are made for several classrooms or groups at one time.*

This book is dedicated to my father,
James R. West,
one of the finest men I have ever known.
Not only is he a wonderful father,
he is also a talented writer.
I believe it is from him that I obtained my skill
with writing as well as the desire to work with words.
I hope that I will be remembered one day,
as he will be,
for being generous, caring, honest, and kind.
Thank you, Dad, for everything.

*Writing a story is simple and fun
when you follow some rules.
You'll have the help that you need
by using writing-process tools.*

A few days ago we learned
how to make our own brainstorming list.
Writing down ideas helps us
avoid those details we may miss.

We also learned that the rough draft
is another thing that you do.
It doesn't matter if it's messy
because that copy's for just you.

Now that we've written our rough draft,
our next step is to edit.
Finding mistakes might make you feel bad,
but only if you let it.

Yel

**One of the things editors do
is to check how words are spelled.
You may have forgotten one of the "e's"
whenever you wrote the word "yelled."**

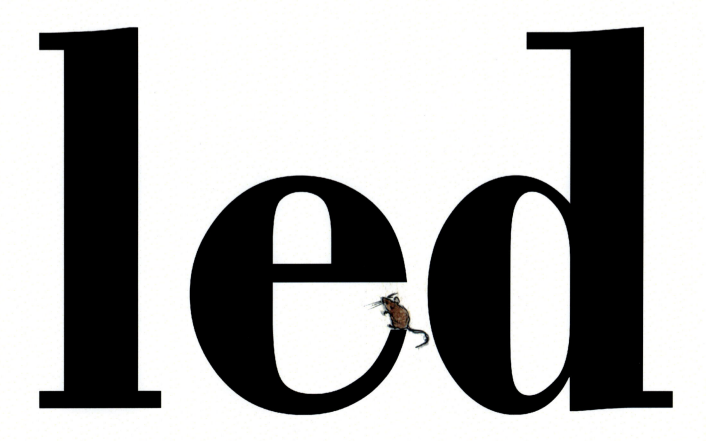

Keep a dictionary by your side;
it can help you when you write.
Some words are really hard to spell
like "elephant" and "fright."

One of the ways to make editing work is to use a brightly colored pen. You should mark on your rough draft to correct what has been.

For example, you may have written a word
you now decide shouldn't be there.
To edit, simply cross out the word
you don't want to share.

Draw three lines under a letter
that should have been upper case.
A slanted line is what you use to mark
where there should be a space.

There are many ways to insert a word
or sentence you forgot.
One of the symbols that some writers use
is called an editing "caret."

*Don't worry about the lines you see
once your editing is complete.
Careful editing will help your story
be one that can't be beat.*

One of the things you're looking for
when you're editing what you've written
is how you spelled all your words -
did you forget the "i" in "mitten"?

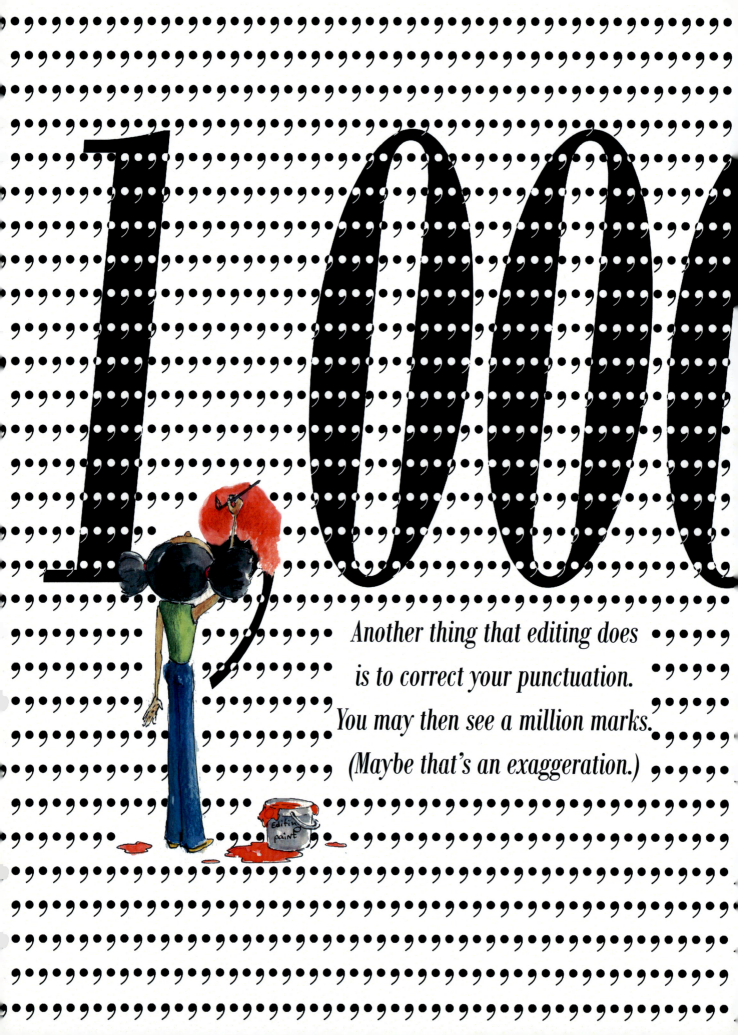

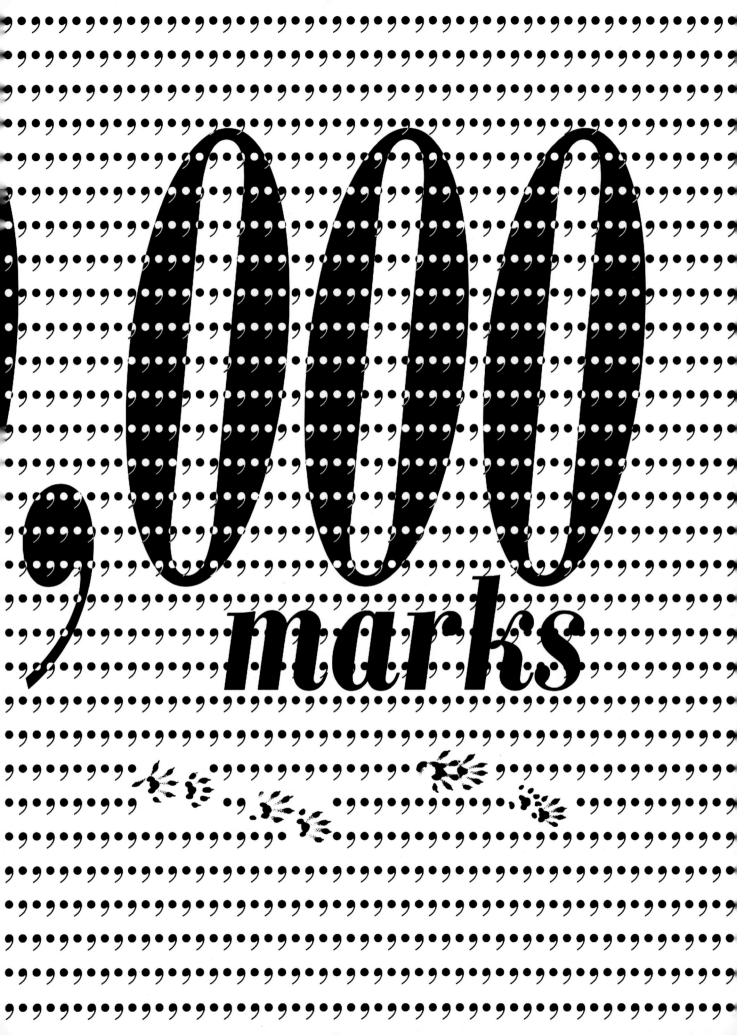

Once you finish the editing job,
your story will be better than before.

If you have time, take a second look and see if you can edit some more

∧ insert

delete

Use the marks on the following page;
they will help you edit right.
And keep this book near you;
don't let it out of your sight.

¶ start new paragraph

∼ transpose letters or words

Editing marks

ߜ	Delete
ⓢⓟ	Spell out word
∧	Change letter
≡	Change to capital letter
lc/	Change to lowercase letter
∼	Transpose letters or words
∧	Insert
⌒	Close space
#	Add space
¶	Start new paragraph

*Now you're ready to revise;
it will make your story shine.*

*Soon you'll proudly tell the world,
"This story is all mine!"*

Other Books
in the Writing is a Process Series,
written by Terri Kelley:

Writing is a Process
Brainstorming: It's Raining Ideas!
Rough Drafts: Bumpy Writing is OK
Conferencing: Let's Talk it Over
Revising: It's Time to Make a Change
Publishing: Finally it's Final!
Presenting: It's Time to Share

Check out other books written by Terri Kelley as well.
They can be purchased from
www.terrikelleybooks.com
as well as from other fine book sellers.
You may also write to Terri
on this site.
She would love
to hear from you.